Opening

Helping children learn about and learn in the primary
school has an important contribution to the lives of
all children – and to wider 'community cohesion' as a whole.
Imaginative teaching and learning about Islam can help children
to see the importance of religion in the lives of Muslims, to counter
stereotypes, and to appreciate what it is that attracts more than
1 billion followers from all parts of world today.

Getting to the heart of what it is to be a Muslim in Britain today
in an open and accessible way is the challenge for good RE.
Enabling children to encounter faith stories, meet believers, ask
questions, and express their own ideas and beliefs in response
to Muslim beliefs is central, as is giving teachers the confidence
to 'have a go' at an area which, for some, feels fraught with
sensitivities. This publication aims to help with both.

On these pages we share some suggestions and practical
activities for exploring Islam and for supporting the subject
leader. As well as focusing on RE outcomes (our main priority!),
cross-curricular links are identified to help schools take learning
about Islam into art, music, literacy and even mathematical
understanding! At all times we aim to ensure the accuracy and
appropriateness of the materials – and we express our thanks to
Nasima Hassan, our faith community consultant, for her help and
advice.

Joyce Mackley

Editor

Web links: RE Today website

The RE Today website offers
subscribers some free additional
resources and classroom ready
materials related to this publication.
Look out for the 'RE Today on the
web' logo at the end of selected
articles.
The password for
access can be found in
each term's
REtoday magazine.

CREATIVE STORYTELLING WITH YOUNGER CHILDREN: FOCUS ON ISLAM

In this section, Marilyn Bowles, an early years specialist from Leicester, describes a creative storytelling approach adapted for use in RE, which she developed with Michelle Green and Kerrie Wood using a NATRE Curriculum Bursary. Further materials from this project can be found on the NATRE website (www.natre.org. uk) where 14 stories, 2 from each of the main faiths and 2 secular stories, can be downloaded.

For the teacher

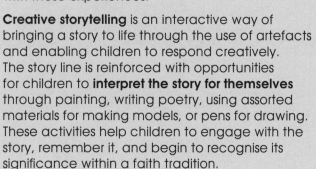

Stories are an integral part of all religious traditions and help to explain and sustain people's belief and faith. Listening to stories is a wonderful way to engage children with these experiences.

Creative storytelling is an interactive way of bringing a story to life through the use of artefacts and enabling children to respond creatively. The story line is reinforced with opportunities for children to **interpret the story for themselves** through painting, writing poetry, using assorted materials for making models, or pens for drawing. These activities help children to engage with the story, remember it, and begin to recognise its significance within a faith tradition.

A Year 1 class come quietly into the storytelling circle, where a lit candle in the centre, quiet music playing and the waiting storyteller set the scene for this shared time.

The approach

The stories are told in a specific way using artefacts and models; a script is used with each story.

At the end of the story there follows some 'I wonder' discussion, followed by an opportunity for the children to create a representation of some part of the story or to make something that the story has made them think about. Two adult teachers/helpers gently support these activities.

The children's creativity is a vital part of the storytelling experience, involving children in an emotional response to what they have heard.

15-20 minutes is set aside for this; then the children come together with their artwork to share in the circle.

Cross-curricular links

Literacy: creative storytelling encourages speaking and listening, shared critical thinking and the use of new vocabulary with the support of artefacts

Art: using materials to create their own work, thinking and talking about the artwork of others

Social development: opportunities for collaborative work.

RE Today
Services

Getting ready for a creative storytelling session

How much time do we need?

An hour is a good time to allow for a creative storytelling session. It's best to run these first thing in the morning or afternoon or after a break time, to allow time for setting up. Make sure enough time is built in to enable children to **create** something worthwhile *and* to **talk about** what they have made at the end of the session. Sharing the children's artistic responses is an essential element.

What resources do we need?

Prepare the creative resources beforehand and place them unobtrusively around the edges of the storytelling place. These could include:

- paint
- assorted papers: large sheets for painting on, sticky tissue and patterned papers for collage
- glue, spreaders
- tablecloths/newspaper for table surfaces
- scissors, crayons, chalks, felt pens, pencils
- playdough, junk modelling materials.

Artefacts: gather together a range of artefacts relevant to the story into an attractive box. Use these to support the telling of the story.

A lit candle at the centre of the circle, with quiet music playing, provides a suitable expectant atmosphere as children arrive.

Who runs the session?

At least two people run the session: one is the **'organiser'** who stands at the door to welcome children into the storytelling space, the other is the **'storyteller'** who sits waiting in the circle for the listeners to gather.

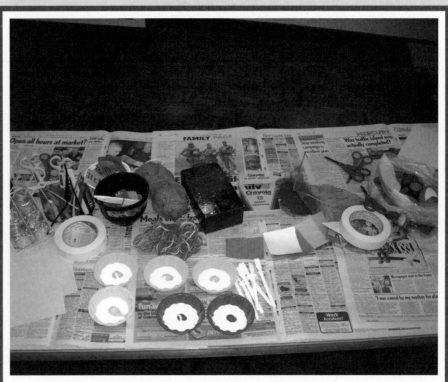

Assorted materials – boxes, papers, beads, buttons with lots of glue – and time and space can produce great results!

Drawing, chalking and crayoning was a popular response to the story with lots of discussion about who was drawing what and why. Zainab chose to use the red shape to the right of her picture (a cave) as the whereabouts of the Prophet Muhammad.

A story from Islam

Age suitability: 3–7 years old

Themes: respect for nature; the example of Muhammad; vandalism

Learning objective: to begin to understand about Muslim beliefs and way of life

Learning outcome: 'I can talk about what I learned from the story about how Muslims behave'.

The boy who threw stones at trees

Once upon a time there was a boy who loved the taste of fresh dates. He lived in a city called Medina where there was a beautiful oasis surrounded by many palm trees. These were date palms. Every day the boy would leave his friends and go to the palm trees where he would take out some stones from his pocket and aim at the trees, trying to get the dates from the trees. He continued to do this until there were lots of dates on the ground; sometimes the dates were not even ripe. The boy never thought about the damage he was doing to the trees and that they might never be able to grow dates again.

One day the farmer who owned the trees noticed that each day there were fewer fruits and that the trees were starting to die. He was very unhappy about this and decided to watch the trees for a whole day. When he saw the boy throwing the stones and trying to steal the unripe dates he was extremely cross and angry. He didn't know what to do with the boy, so he decided to take him to Prophet Muhammad. The boy was frightened. He was usually very well behaved but he so loved fresh dates and it was so easy to knock them down from the trees.

Prophet Muhammad talked very quietly to the boy. He wasn't angry, he knew that the boy hadn't thought about the

trees and that he only did this because of his love for fresh dates. He explained to the boy that he had damaged the trees by throwing stones at them and that if he was patient and waited for the fruit to become ripe, they would be ready to be picked and would taste even better. The boy was upset and said he was sorry to the farmer who forgave him. The boy was very happy to be forgiven and learned to be patient.

Artefacts for the 'story box'

Dates, figures for the boy and the farmer made from wood, plastic or polystyrene; fabric for the 'ground'; stones for rocks for the farmer to hide behind; a school plant for the tree.

Note: The Prophet Muhammad is represented by the movement of the storyteller's hands rather than using a figure.

RE Today
Services

The creative storytelling process: step by step

1 Opening the story box

The storyteller has a **story box** containing the artefacts for use in the telling of the story and a script if needed (see sample script). The storyteller opens the box and reveals its contents, one at a time. For this particular story it might be a piece of coloured fabric to represent a field, a plant to represent the date tree, some stones and dates, and model figures to represent the boy and the farmer.

Figures can be made easily from polystyrene shapes using felt pens for hair, face and features, and fabric glued on for clothing.

2 Setting the story scene

A simple **discussion** is held to set the story scene:

- *'What do you think this fabric might represent?'*

- *'In what way might these stones be used in the story?'*

Praise the children's suggestions and then explain what they do represent (which may of-course be what they suggest). Place them on the floor. The characters are then introduced and placed on the floor.

The contents of 'The boy who threw stones at the date tree' story box

3 Telling the story

During the telling of the story the **artefacts** are used sensitively to bring the story it to life, being moved into position as the story unfolds.

Sample Script

- *'Look at this special box'* (show it to the group).
- *'This box looks like a present doesn't it?'*
- *'It has the 'gift' of a precious story inside.'*
- *'This story has been given to us from the Muslim tradition.'*
- *'Let's look inside and see what story is here.'*
- *'This story is important to Muslims because it teaches them about the wisdom of Allah and Prophet Muhammad and the importance of caring for the natural world.*

4 Following the story

After hearing the story, children are given opportunities to **talk about and express their ideas** from the story.

a Talking together: At the end of the story, the storyteller asks some **'I wonder' questions,** allowing time for children to respond. For example:

- 'I wonder how the boy felt when he was told he'd damaged the date palm?'

- 'I wonder what would have happened if the farmer had not forgiven him?'

- 'I wonder why the Prophet Muhammad suggested this solution to the problem?

- 'I wonder whether you have ever harmed something and regretted it?'

This **philosophical discussion** can embed the children's ideas and spark new learning.

Making time to think ideas through

b Responding to the story: After this discussion there is opportunity for the children to **create a representation** of some part of the story or to make something which the story has made them think about. The two helpers gently support these activities. The children leave the circle one by one to go to **choose their task,** starting with the child to the left of the storyteller. The storyteller stays sitting down as they choose. The **children's creativity** is a vital part of the storytelling experience, involving children in an emotional response to what they have heard. Fifteen or twenty minutes is set aside for this, then the **children come together** with their artwork to share in the circle. To conclude the activity, share a small **'feast'** together: sharing dates from the story, thinking about how dates are a favoured dried fruit for many Muslims, how they grow in hot climates, can be eaten fresh or dried, and are a 'healthy option'!

Harkiran spent a long time forming the date palm, watching other children and then focusing back.

Anesah and Anesu discuss the story as they paint.

Yusuf uses his drawing to explain the 'problem' and how the Prophet Muhammad provided a 'solution.' Yusuf has drawn the Ka'bah in the corner of his picture to show that Allah is there.

RE Today
Services

Another story from Islam:

Age suitability: 3–7 years old
Themes: Forgiveness, saying sorry, honesty
Learning objective: To begin to understand about Muslim beliefs and way of life
Learning outcome: 'I can talk about what I learned from the story about how Muslims behave'.

The woman at the gates of Makkah

There was once a man who sat at the gates into the city of Makkah. His face showed kindness but it also showed lines of sadness and tiredness. One day he saw a woman bustling out of the city gates. She was heavily laden with many bags. The man greeted her and offered to carry some of her bags. The woman was pleased to be helped but explained that he wouldn't want to help her because she was going a long way to the next city. The man said he would still carry her bags for her. 'Why are you leaving Makkah?' he asked the woman. The woman explained that there was a man called Muhammad, making people follow a new religion, worshipping Allah and casting out all the idols they had worshipped before. 'People are mesmerised by him and no one can change their minds. Even slaves who have been tortured and beaten follow him!' explained the woman. The man agreed that some terrible things were happening in Makkah.

As they walked, the woman explained that she was leaving Makkah before she fell under the spell of this man. At last the woman turned to the man and said, 'If only there were more kind people like you in Makkah then I wouldn't have to leave. I'd take your advice. What is your name?'

'My name is Muhammad and I pray to Allah,' replied the man. 'Well', exclaimed the woman, 'there is only one thing left to do.'

'What is that?'

'Would you kindly pick up my bags and carry them back to Makkah with me!'

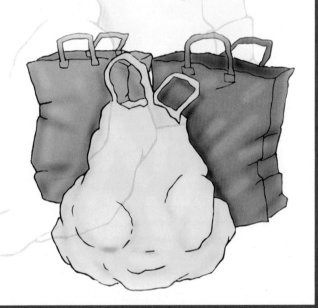

Artefacts for the 'story box'

Figures of a woman with **bags**, bricks for walls of city with a gap for the gate, fabric to represent the path, dried leaves.

Note: The Prophet Muhammad is represented by the movement of the storyteller's hands rather than using a figure.

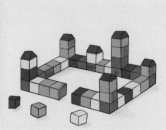 

Other Muslim stories suitable for creative storytelling with younger children can be found in:

- Pages 12 and 13 of this publication

- *My First Quran* by Saniyasnain Khan (Goodword Books 2007) ISBN 978 81-7898-554-1 available from the RE Today online bookshop: www. retoday.org.uk.

- RE Today primary publications: *Faith Stories*, *Stories about God*, *Exploring Sacred Stories* (all ed. J Mackley) www.retoday.org.uk See page 33 for further details.

- www.sln.org.uk/storyboard/stories (Staffordshire learning net website).

What do Muslims believe? Exploring Allah and Muhammad with primary pupils

For the teacher

At the heart of Islam is belief in One God, **Allah**. The existence of God is revealed within nature, and Allah has revealed himself to humankind through his prophets, and finally through Prophet Muhammad.

Muhammad is the 'seal of the prophets', the one through whom God gave his final and unchangeable revelation.

God's word, or revelation, was written down in the **Qur'an** and this is the prime source of knowing how to worship and how to live.

The Qur'an reveals 99 names for **Allah**. Each name tells us something about the nature of God, but even 99 names cannot describe Allah fully.

Approaches for the classroom

There are a number of ways in which teachers can begin to explore the concept of God in Islam with even quite young children.

5–7s:

- Build on 'story' activities such as those described on pages 2–7; the story of Muhammad and the Cat on page 12 is particularly suitable for younger pupils.

- Explore pattern in the natural world and link to the Muslim creation story. *My First Quran* published by Goodword, available from the RE Today bookshop (www.retoday.org.uk) has a lovely version suitable for younger children.

- Think about names and what they tell us about ourselves and about Muslim beliefs about Allah.

7–11s:

- Listen to a Muslim speak about his beliefs through a song; examine the meaning and power behind names and explore the 99 names of Allah;

- Reflect on the big religious question of 'What is God like?' and begin to build up a picture of Muhammad as a real person by reference to stories about him.

What can children do as a result of this unit?

The following pupil-friendly 'I can . . .' statements describe the learning that may be expected of pupils

Level Description of achievement: I can. . .

1
- **recall** a religious story about Allah and Muhammad.
- **use the right words** for things that are special to Muslims, such as the Qur'an.
- **respond** to a question arising from the story.

2
- **retell** a story about Muhammad and say what it tells me about him.
- **pick out** some of the 99 names of Allah and say what they mean.
- **work out some questions** to ask a Muslim.

3
- **describe** some of the 99 names for Allah and say how thinking about these may help someone today.
- **say why** Muslims try to follow Muhammad and have great respect for him.
- **reflect on and express** their own questions and ideas about God.

4
- use the right words to **describe** my understanding of four of the Muslim '99 names' of Allah and **explain** how someone may be influenced by reflecting on these names.
- show that I **understand** how calligraphy expresses some Muslim spiritual ideas.
- refer to Islamic sources or quotations in **giving my own response** to Muslim belief about God.

Cross-curricular links

Music – Islamic nasheed and the work of a Muslim song writer/musician

Literacy – use of faith story, speaking and listening

Art – Islamic artistic expression and calligraphy

SEAL – affirmation exercise building self-esteem.

'I bear witness that. . . there is no God but Allah and that Muhammad is his servant and messenger.'
The Shahada, the First Pillar of Islam

'There is no God but Allah who has the beautiful names'
Qur'an Surah 20.18

RE Today
Services

For the teacher

Good RE enables children to encounter the beliefs and teachings of religions in an authentic and yet accessible, age-appropriate way.

This song was written by Zain Bhiku. He is a well-known Muslim nasheed artist who lives in South Africa but travels all over the world performing his music.

The song can be found on the CD *Children of Heaven*, a compilation of 15 songs for young children. Tracks such as 'Pillars of Islam', 'It's time to Pray' and 'Thank you, Allah' can provide engaging and authentic musical stimulus for key elements of the RE curriculum.

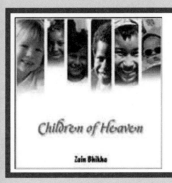

Children of Heaven CD by Zain Bhikha.

CDs by Zain Bhikha are available from www.cdbaby.com

To find out about Zain Bhikha, check out http://www.zainbhikha.com/

Information file

Music and Islam

- **Music is a complicated issue in Islam**, with many different views on what is acceptable. **Some Muslims** believe that **string and wind instruments are haram** (unlawful) and should be forbidden, while **others say percussion is acceptable**. Having become a Muslim, Yusuf Islam (formerly Cat Stephens) turned away from using his guitar. In recent years, however, he has returned to it.

- Throughout history, teachers and scholars have **used rhythm and rhyme** to impart knowledge to their students. **Nasheeds are spiritual songs** which use the rhythms of the human voice unaccompanied by musical instruments.

I am a Muslim

When I was born, the first words that I had heard
Were the words of Allah being whispered through my ear,
And as I felt Allah's power in my soul
That day Islam took me in its fold.

Chorus:

I am a Muslim
Islam my deen
Allah my Lord
His word Qur'an
Muhammad, Prophet
Praise be upon him
I am a Muslim for all of time.

As I grew up, walking in this great big world,
I gazed in awe at the wonders of Allah,
And as I learned the cruel lessons of life
Islam shone through as my guiding light.

Chorus

Look at me now, family around my deathbed,
I know not when Allah will call me home.
The life I led, oh what a blessed thing,
As death comes to me these words I will sing . . .

Chorus

Reproduced by permission of Zain Bhikha Studios

Activities for children

- **Talk about:** What do you think the song is about? If listening, what do you notice about the music?

- **Ask questions:** Imagine you are going to meet Zain – what do you know about him from his song? What questions would you like to ask him?

- **Make a list of any special words** you can see/hear in this song. Talk to a partner and write down what you think these words mean. Compare your ideas with others.

- **Find out about the Adhan** – the words whispered into a newborn Muslim baby's ear. Why do you think Muslim parents do this?

Key words

Islam – comes from the Arabic root, SLM, which means peace, purity, submission and obedience
Muslim – is a follower of Islam - one who submits him/herself to the will of God
Allah – God, creator of the world, the originator of life, the provider of all things in existence
Qur'an – for Muslims the word of God, revealed to Muhammad
Deen: an Arabic word usually translated as 'religion' but also can mean 'way of life'.

Exploring the 99 beautiful names of Allah with children

Engaging pupils' interest

• Children talk about meanings of their own names and whether their names describe what they are like. Talk about nicknames and how these sometimes describe characteristics – sometimes in a nice way, sometimes in a hurtful way.

• Follow this by sharing positive qualities or characteristics. An affirmation exercise in which children write down positive things about each other on a folded sheet of paper passed around the class until all have contributed encourages children to identify these qualities and builds self-esteem in the recipient.

She is a good friend
She is good at maths

Exploring the 99 beautiful names of God in Islam

• **Ask the pupils** if anyone knows the name Muslims (followers of Islam) use for God. **Explain** that Allah is simply the Arabic word for 'God'.

• **Explain** how the Qur'an uses 99 different names for Allah. Each name describes something different about what Allah is like.

• **Ask children** *Why do you think there are 99?* It is not 100. It's to remind Muslims that they don't know everything about God – only Allah knows everything.

Expressing learning and understanding

Pupils could:

• **choose** one name used in the Quran to describe Allah, **reflect** on what the name means, and **think** about how this quality or characteristic might be seen in their own and others' lives today. Sentence starters could be used to support those who need it. Children could decorate their written work with an appropriate Islamic pattern.

• **choose** four of the beautiful names from this page. Copy them in large script. **Explain** what they mean. **Talk or write about** how a person might be changed or influenced by reflecting on each name.

• **look at the way contemporary Islamic artist** Hafeez Shaikh expresses the 99 beautiful names today (http://www.arthafez.com/gallery.html) and be inspired by his use of colour and lettering to **make their own artwork** around the name of God, taking care to follow Islamic principles of not depicting living forms. Using no more than 50 words, children **write a brief statement** explaining their artwork.

Some of the 99 beautiful names of Allah

merciful	supreme
all-peaceful	with-holder
protector	first
mighty	last
king	just
creator	hidden
maker	exalted
provider	generous
judge	patient
all-knowing	guide
watchful	afflicter
gentle	light
forgiving	

One beautiful name found in the Qu'ran for Allah is:

I think it means Allah is. . . . .

If I was. . . . . . I would. . . . .

If other people were. . . . . . they would. . . . .

Activity templates can be downloaded by subscribers from the RE Today website: www.retoday.org.uk

RE Today
Services

AR-RAHIM

The Merciful

He who gives blessings and prosperity, particularly to those who use these gifts as Allah has said, and is merciful to the believers in the hereafter.

YA-RAHMIN

He who repeats this Name 100 times after each Fajr [early morning] prayer will find everyone to be friendly towards him and show easiness to him.

AL-WADUD

The Loving

He who loves those who do good and bestows on them His compassion. He who is the only one who should be loved and whose friendship is to be earned.

YA-WADUD

If there is a quarrel between two people, and one of them repeats this Name 1000 times over some food and has the other person eat the food, there wil be no disagreement between them.

AL-HAKIM

The Wise

He who has wisdom in all orders and actions.

YA-HAKIM

He who repeats this Name continually [from time to time] will not have difficulties in his work.

AL-SALAM

The Source of Peace

He who frees his servants from all danger and obstruction. He who gives His greeting to those fortunate people in heaven.

YA-SALAM

He who repeats this Name 160 times to a sick person will help them regain health.

AL-KHALIQ

The Creator

He who creates every thing from nothing and who creates all things with the knowledge of what will happen to them.

YA-KHALIQ

He who repeats this Name at night Allah will create an angel whose duty it is to act righteously for this person until the day of judgement. The reward for this angel's actions will be given to that person.

AL-HADI

The Guide

He who guides, gives success and directs His servant to do things beneficial to others.

YA-HADI

He who repeats this Name will have spiritual knowledge.

AL-GHAFUR

The All-Forgiving

He who forgives all.

YA-GHAFUR

He who has a headache, fever, and is despondent, who continually repeats this name, will be relieved of his ailment.

AL-KARIM

The Generous One

He who is generous.

YA-KARIM

He who repeats this Name many times will have esteem in this world and the hereafter.

Introducing Muhammad

This unit offers two stories about Muhammad which show his love of Allah's creation and his wisdom. These activities seek to engage pupil's interest and participation through storytelling and the use of everyday objects.

The story of Muhammad and the cat (suitable for younger pupils)

You will need: a toy cat, a piece of material and some scissors.

Place the cat on the cloth.

Tell the story, pausing for pupils to consider what Muhammad might do, and cut the material at the appropriate time.

Talk about:

What do you think about caring for animals?

- If there is a class pet, the pet can be held and questions asked about how it is cared for. Why do people look after animals? Have you ever had to move out of the way because an animal was blocking your way? Did you mind? What did you do? Why?

- Do you think Muhammad was right to cut the cloth? Why do you think he cut it?
  For Early Years children, soft toys can be introduced into a play corner along with feeding utensils, packets of food, combs, brushes, and so on. In the corner a sign can ask 'How would Allah want people to care for these animals?'

A class collage can be created of the mother cat with her kittens sitting upon a piece of material. (Remember Muhammad must not be depicted.) The words, 'Allah cares for all animals' can be written around the cat.

Muhammad and the cat

It was a very hot day. Muhammad sat down in the shade of a date-palm tree and began talking to his friends. He was wearing a long cloak which covered the ground when he sat down. When he went to stand up he noticed that a mother cat had brought her kittens and placed them on the corner of his cloak. The mother started to feed her kittens. Muhammad looked at them and gave thanks to Allah who created all living creatures. Then he . . . .

Pause . . . ask 'What do you think he did?

He asked for a knife. Carefully he cut around his cloak where the cat and her kittens were lying and then without disturbing them he walked quietly away.

RE Today
Services

Muhammad's wisdom

One day the Ka'bah in Makkah was burnt down and it had to be rebuilt. The sacred black stone was kept in a safe place until the Ka'bah had been rebuilt. Different tribes helped to rebuild the Ka'bah but when it came to putting the black stone in place everyone wanted to be the one who placed it there. They started to argue and argue. Finally they agreed that they needed somebody else to be a judge and decide who was important enough to place the black stone in the Ka'bah. Muhammad was chosen.

Muhammad placed a white sheet on the ground, placed the black stone in the middle and asked each of the tribal leaders to hold a side of the sheet and then carry the stone to the right place. Muhammad then fixed the stone in its place. Muhammad became known after that as Al Amin – 'the trustworthy.'

You will need: a 'heavy' load and a large cotton sheet.

Arrange for some pupils to carry the load on a sheet from one end of the room to the other.

The Prophet Muhammad does not appear.

Talk about:

How do you solve arguments? How do you decide what is the truth?

- What sorts of things do you argue about? How do you solve it? Are some ways better than others? How do you decide who is right?
- Why were the people happy with Muhammad's solution?
- Make a list of words to describe Muhammad as he is seen in this story.

Pupils work out an interview with one of the men who held the sheet. The questions include an invitation to make comments about Muhammad and his beliefs. Use a digital video camera to record the interviews and play back to the class.

Assessment opportunities

Pupils could comment upon the style and content of each other's interviews, making sure the focus is on the RE learning outcomes, for example:

- What do you think influenced the actions of Prophet Muhammad?

OPENING UP THE QUR'AN WITH PUPILS

For the teacher

The Holy Qur'an is of central importance in the life of Muslims. This unit provides some activities to help children learn about the Holy Qur'an in the life of Muslims, making links to their own experiences.

The section for 7–9 year olds explores how the Qur'an is precious to Muslims by enabling children to:

• consider what is precious to them

• 'listen' to what Muslims say about the Qur'an

• identify similes for the place of the Qur'an in the life of Muslims.

The section for 9–11 year olds explores the story of the revelation of the Qur'an and picks up on ideas about asking big questions, standing up for the truth, and facing opposition and injustice, making links to children's own experiences.

What can children do as a result of this unit?

The following pupil-friendly 'I can . . .' statements describe the learning that may be expected of pupils.

Level Description of achievement: I can. . .

3
• **use some religious words** to **describe** how important the Qur'an is to Muslims, and say how Muslims treat the Qur'an because of this.
• *make links* to my own feelings about something precious to me.

4
• show that I **understand** some ways in which Muslim beliefs about the Qur'an can affect their everyday lives
• come up with some *thoughtful questions* that arise through learning about the 'Night of Power'; *suggest some answers* to at least four questions.

5
• give at least three **reasons why** Laylat al Qadr is so important to individual Muslims and to the Muslim community.
• *explain* what inspires me to stand up for what I believe in and how difficult it can be.

Information file: The Holy Qur'an and Islam

Muslims believe that the Qur'an

• was a gift from God, revealed by the Angel Jibril (Gabriel) to God's messenger, the Prophet Muhammad.

• is a copy of a book kept in heaven – and it contains God's guidance on what to believe and how to live good lives. The Qur'an is precious to Muslims because of this and they show how important it is by:

  ° reading and studying it. Muslim children often learn Arabic so that they can read the Qur'an. Some Muslims learn all of the 112 chapters or surahs of the Qur'an by heart. These Muslims are called *Hafiz*. Hafiz are highly respected people as they have a memorised record of God's words.

  ° treating their copies with care, making sure it is covered, washing their hands before using it, placing it on a stand rather than on the table (and never on the floor), and placing it high up when they are not using it to show that it is better than other books.

The guidance in the Qur'an is taken very seriously by Muslims because it comes from the highest authority – Allah, the creator. Many Muslims find that reciting the Qur'an helps them to be calm. It helps them to see what is important in life. It reminds them that God is looking after them, and that they should try and do what he wants, and that this is what will make them happy.

RE Today Services

Something precious: classroom activities for 7–9s

You will need:
- An English translation of the Qur'an or a book of stories from the Qur'an (see note below)
- A Qur'an stand and two cloths
- Something that is precious to you personally.
- Statement cards from page 16 (enough for each pair of children to have a pack).

1   A mystery package . . .
Seat children in a circle around a low table covered with a cloth. On the table there should be a wrapped Qur'an (English version) or book of stories from the Qur'an on a stand, with a cloth covering everything. Allow a sense of mystery to develop around this.

2   Something precious to you . . .
When the children are settled, bring out the object that is precious to you. Explain why it is so special – perhaps who gave it to you, what it reminds you of, where you keep it. Ask children how they think you treat your precious object and how you would like them to treat it.

3   Something precious to them . . .
Allow the children to talk in pairs for a few minutes about something that is precious to them – talk about where it came from, why it is precious, how they treat it. You may ask for a few examples to be shared with the rest of the group.

4   Something precious to . . . whom?
Now introduce the idea that you are going to see something that is very precious to many people in the world – perhaps some in your class too. Take off the cloth and reveal the wrapped Qur'an on the stand. Ask children if they know what it is, or if they can say what they think it is.

5   Unwrapping the Qur'an . . .
With great care unwrap the Qur'an and place it on the stand. Ask children what these actions show about the book. To whom is the book precious? How should we treat a book that is sacred to others? See if they can make links between their own precious things and this.

(Mention that **'sacred'** is a word that means something like 'precious', but that it is used for things that are set apart or dedicated in religions – usually things that come from God or are used in worship of God. **'Holy'** is a similar term, often applied to things that are regarded with awe.)

6   Muslims say . . .
Explain that children are to 'hear' from some people for whom this book is sacred/holy. What these people say is written on the cards.

- Ask children, in pairs, to take a pack of cards.
- Ask children to read each card carefully – taking it in turns to read out loud to each other.
- Ask children to pick out the main thing the person says on the card – a key word or phrase.
- Ask children to record this on the paper – numbering down the page from 1 to 6 – with the key phrase alongside each number.

7   Showing understanding . . .
After 15–20 minutes, or when most have completed this stage, ask children to form groups of four or eight to share their findings. Use this information to write a group statement beginning: **The Qur'an is precious for Muslims because . . .**

Follow up this activity by looking at Qur'an metaphors (page 17).

Using the Qur'an with children
It is recommended that you use an English translation of the Qur'an or a book of stories from the Qur'an rather than an Arabic version in the classroom. This is because:

- it is more accessible to children and parents
- Islam is a global religion and many faith members use an English version
- the Arabic version is the most sacred text and offence may be caused for some parents if it is used in a 'show and tell' type of activity.

The Holy Qur'an is precious to me because . . .

. . . **it is the teaching of Allah.**

Imran

. . . the Prophet Muhammad received the Qur'an as a gift from Allah, the Creator and Sustainer of the World.

Tufael

. . . it is a complete guide, guiding me through my life and how it should be led as a Muslim.

Samreena

. . . the Qur'an contains the truth to be followed by Muslims. It says in it that it is 'a book which has been revealed, in order that mankind can be led out of the depths of darkness into light'.

(Qur'an Surah 14)

Rafiah

Wasim with his Qur'an

. . . it is like the direct spoken words of Allah recorded on paper. The Arabic words mean more to me than any other words in any other book.

Razwan

. . . I can read the Qur'an, even though it is in Arabic! I've had special lessons to help me learn Arabic. The Qur'an tells us how to live. If I follow the Qur'an I could become a good person as the Qur'an is a book given to us from Allah.

Wasim

. . . I use the Qur'an as a guidance on problems with everyday life. Everybody needs to turn to someone sometime – why not turn to a higher authority?

Timothy

. . . the Qur'an teaches me how to live my life well. It teaches me to:

- be kind to my parents
- keep promises and agreements
- be honest
- avoid gossip and slander
- avoid being wasteful
- avoid taking advantage of poor people
(Qur'an Surah 17)

Jasmina

RE Today Services

Activity: Qur'an similes – deepening learning for 7–9s

1 **This is a sorting activity aimed at making sense of the place of the Qur'an in the life of a Muslim.**

The following similes are some of the ways a Muslim might describe the Qur'an. Copy and cut up the text cards. Give children a set each of the pink statements and the green statements. Ask them to match the correct endings (from the green cards) to the sentence starters in the left-hand column (pink).

2 **Ask children to try to create some Qur'an similes for themselves.** Write them in the same format as those below. Examples could include: 'The Quran is like: meat/ a football manager/ a minaret/a lion/water/jewels', etc.

These similes can be related to what Muslims say about the Qur'an, e.g. as a straight path; as the truth; as a guide; as the gift of Allah; as the final Revelation.

For a Muslim, the Qur'an might be like a lighthouse because . . .		. . . it can challenge you to do your very best.
For a Muslim, the Qur'an might be like a special teddy bear because . . .		. . . it is deep and can take a lifetime to explore.
For a Muslim, the Qur'an might be like a target because . . .		. . . it can help you get through stormy times.
For a Muslim, the Qur'an might be like a teacher because . . .		. . . it can tell you when you're doing wrong and help you do right.
For a Muslim, the Qur'an might be like a police officer because . . .		. . . it can make you feel safe when you are afraid.
For a Muslim, the Qur'an might be like an ocean because . . .		. . . it doesn't always reveal its secrets easily.
For a Muslim, the Qur'an might be like an Old Master (painting) because . . .		. . . it can give you something to aim for.
For a Muslim, the Qur'an might be like a Magic Eye picture because . . .		. . . it is the work of a great Creator and is always best in the original.

3 **Ask children to identify things or people that help them in the way the Qur'an helps Muslims.**

For example:

- *Who is like a lighthouse to you?*
- *What helps you to get through stormy times?*
- *What do you know that is deep and worth exploring?*

4 **Ask children to write another sentence starting 'The Qur'an is precious to Muslims because . . .'**

Share children's responses and agree together which are the most thoughtful answers. Have children 'gone deeper' as a result of their further learning?

RE Today
Services

Using the story of the 'Night of Power' – the revelation of the Holy Qur'an

The story of the 'Night of Power' is a key Muslim story of the way in which the Qur'an was first revealed to Muhammad. A version of the story can be found on page 19. Try some or all of the following activities to engage children in thinking about and responding to the story.

1   Stop and think!

Muhammad was shocked by the injustice, exploitation, poverty, suffering and idol worship he encountered in Makkah. It 'stopped him in his tracks'.

In pairs children talk about:

- what kinds of things 'stop you in your tracks', or make you 'stop and think'?
- what things amaze you?
- what things bother or upset you?

Report back to the class.

As a class: Draw up a list of the positive and negative responses. Which are the most amazing or the most upsetting?

2   Questions, questions

Muhammad's experiences made him ask many questions about life, about God, about how to live a good life.

- What big questions do pupils have? Use the list of amazing and upsetting things from Task 1 to get the pupils to generate questions.
- Sort them into closed and open questions. Which questions are the big questions of life?
- Put these questions on large sheets of paper around the room. Ask pupils to have a go at answering some of them on sticky notes and stick these on the sheets. Gather their responses and discuss the suggestions.

3   Getting away from it all

Muhammad left the pressures and tensions of the city and went to the quiet and solitude of the cave in the mountains.

In pairs pupils talk about:

- Where can you go to think?
- Do you have a special place where you go to sort things out? What's it like? How would you describe it to someone who's never been?
- How do you feel when you are there?
- Why is it important to think things through?

Pupils might like to design a spiritual garden for the school – a place to stop and think about things that really matter.

4   Telling others

Explore with pupils the cost for Muhammad 'the truth'.

- Use the newspaper account to work out who might be most likely to listen to Muhammad and who might be most likely to reject his message. Why might they do this, and how might they show their responses? (Pupils may do some research about this.)
- Explore the difficulty of standing up for the things you believe in – for example, telling the truth, doing the right thing. Some contemporary examples might be: telling the truth even though you may get into trouble; admitting that you like a certain team or band; saying no to friends when they are trying to get you to be naughty, and so on.

5   Celebrating that night!

Muslims believe that the Night of Power – Laylat al-Qadr – was the start of the revelation of the Holy Qur'an. One verse in the Qur'an promises that prayer on this night is worth 1000 months of worship (Surah 97).

In groups, pupils could:

- **suggest** five ways in which they think Muslims would celebrate this important event.
- **talk about:** why Muslims would celebrate it.
- **find out** what Muslims actually do to celebrate Laylat al Qadr.

RE Today
Services

Makkah Times

A Mighty Night

Holy Message Revealed to Muhammad

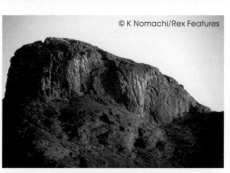
© K Nomachi/Rex Features

Mount Hira

Muhammad, 40, a trusted merchant from Makkah, has received a revelation from God, according to his respected wife, Khadijah. Al-Ameen (The Truthful One), as he is known, told his wife about what happened to him in the cave at Mount Hira, three miles north of the city.

One God

Muhammad has always disagreed with the way that people of Makkah worship lots of gods. He chooses to worship the one God, Allah, often spending time in prayer and meditation at Hira. He has always been unhappy with the fighting between tribes and the unfair treatment of the poor. He hates the worship of useless gods and goddesses. He recently spent the month of Ramadan in prayer at Hira, pondering questions about God, life, justice and truth.

Night of Power

One night when he was alone in the cave at Hira, he had a strange feeling, as though someone else was there! An immense voice echoed around the cave. 'Recite!' Muhammad saw that it was an angel, who commanded him again, 'Recite!' At first Muhammad said, 'I cannot read!' but a third time the angel commanded him to read.

The First Revelation

Muhammad's mind became clear. He found that he could understand the words the angel spoke and that he could recite them out loud. He realised that the message was from the one God, Allah, and it burned on his heart.

The Messenger

Shaken by his experience, Muhammad left the cave. As he left, he heard a voice again: 'O Muhammad, you are the messenger of Allah, and I am the angel Jibril.'

Facing the World

Returning to his wife, Khadijah, Muhammad told her everything that had happened. She wrapped him in a coat to comfort him and told him not to worry – he was not crazy, but that he had an important message from God for all people. Muhammad has started to tell the people of Makkah – but not everyone is pleased with his message.

The Story Continues

Muhammad has returned to the cave and received several more messages. The revelation seems to be continuing. His friends and family are beginning to record the words on scraps of pottery and fabric – anything that comes to hand.

Ka'bah Idols for Sale

The valuable market in idols is growing fast. Based at the holy shrine, the Ka'bah, the place of pilgrimage for many people, the selling of idols is bringing in lots of money for some of the rich tribal leaders in the city. Since they believe in lots of gods, there are lots of idols to sell!

• • • • • • • • •

Trouble in Makkah

Warring tribes around Makkah have clashed again in the city. They are arguing over who gets the most money from the trade in idols. Several people were killed in the violence – and the death toll from the years of rivalry increases almost daily.

• • • • • • • • •

Messenger Rejected

Many people, including members of his own family, are not happy with the message of Muhammad. Whilst some are calling him 'The Prophet of God', others are angry that he is challenging their ideas about the gods of Makkah. Some of them have been attacking the followers of Muhammad, who is warning them that Allah is their Creator but also their Judge.

RE Today Services

19

EXPLORING PATTERN AND SHAPE IN ISLAM

For the teacher

- **Tawhid** (the Oneness of Allah) is central to Islam. This fundamental, and profound, concept is expressed in a variety of ways in everyday life, some of which are very accessible to young children.

- This article focuses on how Tawhid is expressed through **pattern and shape**, and the **design of gardens**.

RE syllabus links

- The activities will contribute to work exploring how religious beliefs are expressed and understood by believers, and provide opportunities for pupils to explore questions related to belief in God in an imaginative and creative way.

- There are also opportunities for learning outside the classroom, in the creation of a garden based on Muslim principles, whether on a grand scale or in miniature.

Cross-curricular links

These RE activities make a significant contribution to:

- understanding the arts: the insights of different cultures

- mathematical understanding – patterns

- learning and thinking skills – using imagination to think creatively and generate ideas.

What can children do as a result of this unit?

The following pupil-friendly 'I can . . .' statements describe the learning that may be expected of pupils. Level 3 describes what most 8–9 year olds should be able to do.

Level Description of achievement: I can. . .

2
- **identify** two things Muslims believe about God.
- **suggest** two questions about God which are interesting and hard to answer.

3
- **describe** a Muslim belief about God.
- **make a simple link** between my ideas and questions about God and some Muslim ideas.

4
- show that I **understand** the word 'Tawhid' for myself.
- **create a statement** of my own beliefs and questions about God referring to ideas from the Muslim ideas I have studied.

See also

1 Taprats: Taprats is a free Java applet which generates Islamic star patterns. It can be used online or downloaded onto your computer. Instructions are provided, but basic use is intuitive. www.cgl.uwaterloo.ca/~csk/washington/taprats

2 Gardens of the Islamic World, REEP: 'Gardens of the Islamic World' is a comprehensive overview of the main features of Islamic gardens. It is well illustrated, and there are links to useful websites: www.reep.org

3 *Islamic Designs (British Museum Pattern Book):* an extensive collection of designs in black and white (Eva Wilson, British Museum Press, 2001, ISBN 978-0-7141-8066-3).

4 Pattern in Islamic Art: This website offers a free download of over 4000 images of patterns and other design features drawn from the Muslim world. The slideshow on the home page offers a useful classroom resource – what do pupils notice as the images scroll through? www.patterninislamicart.com

5 *Inspiring Visual RE: Using and Making Art in Primary RE:* a collection of tried and tested curriculum activities, including a section on using art from Islam (ed. Joyce Mackley, RE Today 2009, ISBN 978-1-905893-24-9). www.retoday.org.uk

6 Art Hafez: A stimulating gallery of work by the artist Hafeez Sheikh, who aims to use his talents to develop the use of Islamic art in various aspects of daily life. www.arthafez.com

RE Today Services

© Eva Wilson

From Eva Wilson, *Islamic Designs*, British Museum Pattern Books 1988; the image appears by kind permission of Eva Wilson.

To think about

Look carefully at the two pictures on this page.

1 What shapes do you see?

2 What do you notice about the shapes, and the patterns they create?

3 If these shapes and patterns say something about what a person believes – what might those beliefs be?

4 Where might you see shapes and patterns like these?

Activity 1

Ask children to:

- **look closely** at the two patterns on page 21, and respond to the prompt questions alongside.

- **suggest** what sorts of beliefs the shapes and patterns might represent – about God? Creation? Life? What reasons can they give for their ideas?

- **reflect** – if they were to represent something really important to themselves in a shape or pattern, what shape or pattern would they choose, and why?

Explain:

- the shapes they see (squares, circles, etc) are used by Muslims to express some of their most important beliefs.

- the circle is regarded as the perfect shape, as it has no beginning and no end. It means infinity (distance that has no end), eternity (time that has no end), oneness or unity. The circle also stands for Allah (God).

Activity 2

Each of the nine cards on page 23 provides a quotation from the Qur'an or a young Muslim which expresses an important Muslim belief.

Ask children to:

- **choose** the cards which they think match up with their ideas about the meaning of the shapes for Muslim beliefs they identified in Activity 1, e.g. the circle matches with the statement that Allah is One.

- **suggest** which colours might be used in particular to express the beliefs they identified.

- **reflect** – what advantages might shapes, patterns and colours have over words or actions in expressing what really matters?

Explain:

For Muslims, certain colours have particular meaning:

- **black:** the colour of Prophet Muhammad's family.
- **blue:** the colour of infinity and revelation.
- **green:** the colour of paradise, and of Islam.
- **white:** the colour of purity.
- **yellow:** the colour of glory, plenty, and continuity.

Activity 3

Ask children to:

- **use** the Taprats applet (see page 20) to create Islamic star patterns. Encourage children to appreciate and talk about how, from a few basic shapes, great diversity and variety can be created.

- **suggest** what links Muslims might see between the shapes they have created using Taprats, and the beliefs of Tawhid (the Oneness of Allah) and creation.

- **reflect:** what questions do they have for Muslims about their beliefs about God? How might a Muslim visitor to their class answer their questions? What ideas and questions about God do pupils have for themselves? How might they express them in shape, design, colour and/or words?

The work of Muslim artist Hafeez Sheikh may provide useful stimulus to thinking – how does his art express his beliefs? See: www.arthafez.com

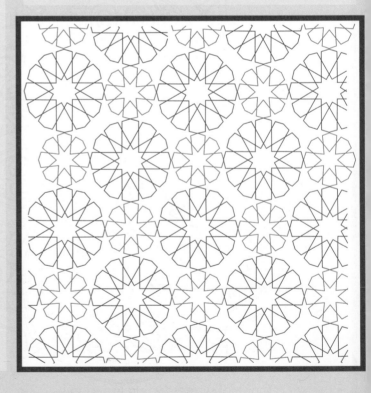

Expressing belief: Islamic gardens

Tawhid I think God is merciful and helpful to other people when they need help. God is the most powerful, and is one. Muslim girl, aged 10	**Tawhid** He is Allah, The One and Only; Allah, the Eternal, Absolute; He begot none, nor was he begotten; And there is none like Him. Qur'an, surah 112:1-4	**Tawhid** God is most powerful. He is not born, and does not give birth. He is the first and the last and he can destroy and bring back to life. Muslim girl, aged 11
Paradise (Jannah) In [the Garden] are rivers of water . . . rivers of milk . . . rivers of wine . . . and rivers of honey. Qur'an, surah 47:15	**Paradise (Jannah)** The Prophet said, 'There is a tree in Paradise which is so big and huge that if a rider travels in its shade for one hundred years, he would not be able to cross it.' Hadith – Sahih Bukhari 4:474	**Paradise (Jannah)** When I die God will ask me what have I done bad and what I have done good. If I did more good things I will go to Paradise. If I did more bad things I will go to hell. Muslim boy, aged 10
Gardens God promises to believers gardens underneath which rivers flow, where they will live. Qur'an, surah 9:72	**The Shahadah** (Declaration of faith) There is no god but Allah, and Muhammad is the Messenger of Allah.	**Creation** To Him is due the origin of the heavens and the earth. When He decrees a matter, He says to it 'Be', and it is. Qur'an, surah 2:117

Activity 4

Ask children to:

- **suggest** what they think a 'peaceful garden' would look like, and why.

- **compare** their ideas with those of Muslims. Display pictures of Islamic gardens (see www.reep.org) – or use the diagram on page 24. What similarities and differences do they notice? What reasons can they suggest?

- **make links** between the statements on the nine cards above and the features of Muslim gardens they identified.

- **reflect** – How important are gardens are for human beings, however they are designed?

Explain:

- the importance of symmetry, circles, squares, hexagons, the number 8 and certain colours for Muslims (see Activities 1 and 2).

Activity 5

Ask children to:

- **research** and **design** a garden suitable for the grounds of a mosque. Background information and ideas for the classroom can be found at www.reep.org and the diagram on page 24 will also be helpful.

- **explain** the reasons for their design, showing understanding of key Muslim beliefs and design principles. Could they persuade the Imam at the mosque to choose their design?

- **reflect** – what benefits might a school garden have for pupils and teachers? What design can they suggest?

Consider:

- creating a Muslim garden 'for real' – either in miniature (e.g. in a window box) or on as large a scale as school grounds permit. Detailed guidance can be found at www.reep.org.

Key features of Islamic gardens

Plants

Flower beds are always a geometric shape, e.g. rectangle, star shape (usually 8-pointed), diamond or octagon.

Paths

Paths are usually paved in a geometric design. Raised paths run alongside water channels in large gardens.

Water channels

These are always straight and shallow, and often tiled in jade or turquoise. Sometimes small fountains line the channels.

Number eight

The number eight is associated with Paradise in Islam. How many examples of 'eight' can you find?

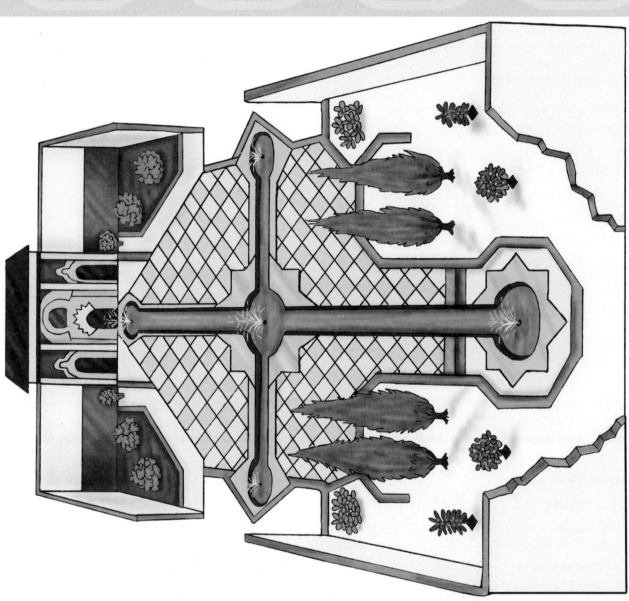

Walls and screens

Gardens often have a wall or screen around them, making them private.

Trees

Italian cypress trees are popular. Fruit trees can be used. Mulberry, rowan and hawthorn suit the British climate.

Water

Water is at the heart of an Islamic garden. Pools are always geometric in shape, and many small fountains are common.

Unity

Gardens are symmetrical, and carefully put together to create a sense of harmony and peace.

RE Today
Services

WHAT DOES IT MEAN TO BE A MUSLIM IN BRITAIN TODAY?

For the teacher

It is fascinating to see how British Muslim children practise their faith, and to trace the impact of their identity on their lives. This set of lesson ideas uses original material from young British Muslims to enable any child in the 7–11 age range to understand the practice of the faith and to open up the possibility of learning from Islam.

Forty quotations from Muslims in Britain aged from 7 to 14 are the basic resource. There are:

- eight quotations about each of the Five Pillars of Islam
- four different activities, each using a different thinking skill
- a structure for pupils' own reflection on their own intentions, choices and ambitions.

Making a mini model mosque (template provided on page 30) opens up opportunities for pupils to think about worship and community. Get them to ask five questions of their own about the model, and how it is used, then plan an enquiry to find answers.

Making the mini model mosque

a Cut out the model and its parts first. Score fold lines with a biro and ruler.

b Colour all the pieces. You could, for example, put yellow in the windows for light, and colour all four of the 'dome' sections on both sides.

c Stick the sections together – minaret, mihrab, prayer hall (Zullah).

d Fit the two parts of the larger dome together so that they intersect along the cut lines, and stick to the prayer hall roof where indicated by the dotted lines.

e Stick the circle on top of the minaret and stick the smaller dome on top.

f Stick the minaret and the mihrab to the prayer hall.

g Lastly, secure the model to the base.

h Add some finishing touches. Use the Islamic garden picture to design a courtyard for your model.

What can children do as a result of this unit?

This work can make a major focus for assessing what pupils have learned about Islam and learned from Islam. The following pupil-friendly 'I can . . .' statements describe the learning that may be expected of pupils.

Level Description of achievement: I can. . .

1
- **talk about** what Muslim people do in their religion.
- **talk about** something that I do that matters to me.

2
- **recognise** three ways in which Muslim people try to follow Allah.
- **respond sensitively** to some of the feelings Muslims experience through their practice of Five Pillars.

3
- **describe** what Muslims do to practise the Five Pillars.
- **make links** between Muslim intentions and ambitions and my own intentions and ambitions.

4
- **use the right words** to show that I **understand** how following the Five Pillars gives strength and shape to Muslim life.
- **apply** ideas like duty, intention, determination or belief to Muslim ways of life and to my own way of life.

Note: The Five Pillars of Islam are not all of equal significance. Belief in Allah and the Prophets comes first. The fifth pillar is not optional. The pillars each have an interesting time dimension to their practice: *believe* every moment, *pray* five times daily, *give* when you do your accounts, *fast* for a month out of the year, *travel* to Makkah once in a lifetime if you can.

The work can be assessed using the template at the top of page 29 (it is good to enlarge it to a bigger size). This asks pupils to think carefully about their own lives in the light of their learning about Islam. Get them to use the sheet to record initial ideas, then discuss the different ideas they have come up with in a group, before working to redraft a final, thoughtful page. The final row of the template often shows achievement at level 4 if it is done thoughtfully.

Forty bricks to build the Five Pillars of Islam: four activities

1 Sorting for thinking: Copy and cut out a set of the cards on this and the following pages for each group of four pupils. Sets done on different colours of card can be stored in an envelope. Ask the children to begin by sorting the cards. There are eight that relate to each of the Five Pillars: belief, prayer, giving, fasting and pilgrimage. They should lay out their set on a table, like a pillar.

2 Ranking for thinking: Ask pupils to re-read the cards (when sorting, they will have looked very quickly at the text). This time, they should rank the cards. Which ones make the most interesting or important points about the Pillars?

3 Raising questions and suggesting answers myself: Give pupils a choice – they can select six of the cards each in their groups – quotations they find interesting. Individually, they write down a question they would like to ask the person who made the comment. As a group, they suggest answers to the questions they think Muslim young people would give.

4 Reflecting on my own life: Ask pupils next to take five blank cards of their own (shape and colour these like bricks). Ask pupils to write on each card an example of what makes them feel strong, what gives strength to their lives. A class of 30 will write 150 'bricks'. These might be what makes the class strong. Discuss (in circle time?) whether these bricks are like the 50 bricks about the Muslim Pillars which give strength to the faith.

Display idea: Make a display for the school entrance hall, using the Muslim 'bricks' and the class's 'bricks' to show similarities and differences between sources of strength in Islam and in your class. Invite other teachers and visitors to the school to contribute a brick of their own (Ofsted will find this idea irresistible).

God is one. We worship.

On the Day of Judgement, two angels will give our record books to Allah, and Allah will be deciding who will enter Paradise.

I believe in the Day of Judgement, I think it is interesting. In the Qur'an it says we will be resurrected and asked many questions by the angel. One is 'What is your religion?'

For Muslims, faith provides a chance to live a life under the guidance of Allah. If you begin with the name of Allah, then Allah will help you.

For the good person, the grave will be like your mother hugging you, and will turn into a heaven much bigger.

Our religion is Islam, we believe in only one God, who is Allah. And Muhammad is the last prophet. Being Muslims, we follow Muhammad and worship Allah.

I believe that the Prophet Muhammad was sent from Allah. He was a very honest and reliable person: even a non-believer called him Sadiq (which means trustful).

When worshipping, think about who you are worshipping. Have faith in what you have been taught. Nobody is worthy of worship except Allah.

When you give money away, you're not thinking 'I could have spent that.' You're thinking 'Allah has been good to me.' It makes you thankful.

RE Today Services

Fasting places a strain on some school days, for instance when you're playing sport you tend to get thirsty. But I believe this is a small price to pay for fulfilling my duties as a Muslim.

Prayer should help us to stop doing evil. It is something solemn, not a joke. It should make us feel close to Allah, just as if He is right there in front of us.

GIVING IS GOOD.

Islamic Relief is a big Muslim charity which uses our Zakat to help those who are needy all over the world.

It is very difficult to describe exactly how prayer makes me feel. One feeling is being refreshed, and ready to carry on with the rest of the day. Also that God is there for me and will forgive me if I should do something wrong.

When I pray, I feel very relaxed and happy, especially on the Friday Prayer, which keeps us Muslims together and united.

It makes me feel strength in my faith, and develops a united community.

One of my uncles was very poor when he first came to Britain, and he was given money to help him from the mosque. He is well off now, and the most generous man I know.

It gives you better discipline and moral stature if you pray five times a day. However, some people are lazy and miss their prayers. Unfortunately one of those idle people is me.

For the good person, the grave will be like your mother hugging you, and will turn into a heaven much bigger.

Friday prayer emphasises the feeling of Ummah, of brotherhood and equality. No distinctions are made in prayer.

Money isn't everything. This pillar reminds us of all the best things in life, and to help the needy. It disciplines you.

Prayer makes me feel more lively and responsible, a new person inside.

The prayer makes me feel that I communicate with God.

The Prophet said that whoever is good to the poor pleases God.

This pillar is a training programme in which I feel for the poor, plus I can try and help.

I do observe Ramadan for thirty days, because that's what our Prophet did, and he obeyed Allah. Ramadan is very important to Muslims because it is the month when the glorious Qur'an was revealed.

We fast to remember the poverty in the poorer countries of the world, and how we could help by giving money. It makes us thankful to God.

Id-ul-Fitr is my favourite day in the whole year. I meet most of my cousins in the mosque, greeting each other with 'salam'. Every Muslim in the world will be celebrating our Holy Prophet Muhammad. It's the day after Ramadan, and the Imam does a beautiful speech.

We like to give Zakat because we get the feel of how it is for poor people when they have no food to eat, and we realise not to waste.

EACH YEAR IN RAMADAN, I LEARN A NEW THING ABOUT MYSELF, AND I ALSO GET RID OF AT LEAST ONE BAD TRAIT IN MYSELF. IT TEACHES SELF-CONTROL, WHICH IS VERY BADLY NEEDED AMONG US HUMANS.

In Hajj, people go and circulate the Holy Ka'bah and they do not pull a single hair out, or kill any fly or insect. You feel happy that you are pleasing Allah. I have heard people say that on Hajj they feel at ease, because they know Allah is there with them.

I think Makkah is beautiful: there you can worship Allah from your heart, and ask for forgiveness. I have never been to Makkah, but I have great emotions about the city. I am going to make sure I get a chance to visit Makkah, Insh'Allah.

The most important thing to me about pilgrimage is that the Holy Prophet has stood on the soil of Makkah.

At the end of Ramadan, I have mixed feelings: achievement and regret. I thank God that I've been able to keep my fasts, but I regret not having done better, especially in improving my behaviour.

I feel very happy when I hear about Makkah: this city is important to us because it is the oldest place of worship, and our Holy Prophet was born here. I have been to the sacred city, and it made me cry when I first saw how beautiful the Ka'bah was in reality.

Makkah is very important because it's a meeting place for the whole human race. I would like to see where the Prophet stood and preached.

Insh'Allah I have been keeping the fast for seven years now. Ramadan is a month in which you and your Lord are very close.

I think Ramadan is a good event. If you fast you become very aware of yourself and very God-conscious too.

I went on Hajj when I was 12. It was very big, with people there from all over the world, many different countries, races and colours. I was amazed Nobody did bad things like hit each other or steal

My Dad has been to Makkah. He says it's important because all Muslims around the world come together, not interested in their colour, language or wealth, but united as brothers and sisters in their religion.

When I went, I saw the Ka'bah. It felt like I just wanted to run towards it, and submit.

RE Today Services

Muslim practice: the Five Pillars (AT1)	My own intentions and plans for my life (AT2)
Every moment, Muslims believe . . .	Every moment, I believe . . .
Five times a day, Muslims try to . . .	Each day, I want to try . . .
When their money comes in, Muslims like to . . .	If I chose to be generous, I would . . .
For one month in the year, Muslims . . .	In the next year, I intend to . . .
Once in a lifetime, Muslims hope to go . . .	One big hope for my lifetime is . . .

Similarities and differences between my intentions and Muslim intentions

Using this material with younger children: four simple ideas for deeper learning

1 **Talking Pillars in circle time:** Choose a smaller number of the cards: say 15 or 20 instead of 40. Select those that are simpler to read or to understand. Ask pupils to take one card and make a picture to go with it. Set out the cards in circle time and use them for a speaking and listening session: What do Muslims do? And why do they do these things?

2 **Mini model mosques:** Enlarge the card net on page 30 to double or three times its size, and get pupils to work together to make the model: this is easier than making a tiny one individually, and the bigger models can be 'filled'. (Instructions can be found on page 25.) Ask children: what would you see, hear and touch in the mosque? Get them to make simple card or lego artefacts to go inside.

3 **Feelings at worship:** Ask pupils to think about what cannot be seen in the mosque: for example peace, atmosphere, devotion, thoughtfulness, the presence of Allah. What words would they also like to put in the model mosques? What symbols (not pictures) would show the deeper meaning of the building?

4 **SEAL links:** Make a link to work from the social and emotional aspects of learning in this activity. Ask children to talk about the times when they feel peace, unity, happiness, amazement, regret, generosity, and some of the other feelings mentioned in the '40 bricks'.

Make a mini model mosque

Colour the domes on both sides
and decorate windows and walls.

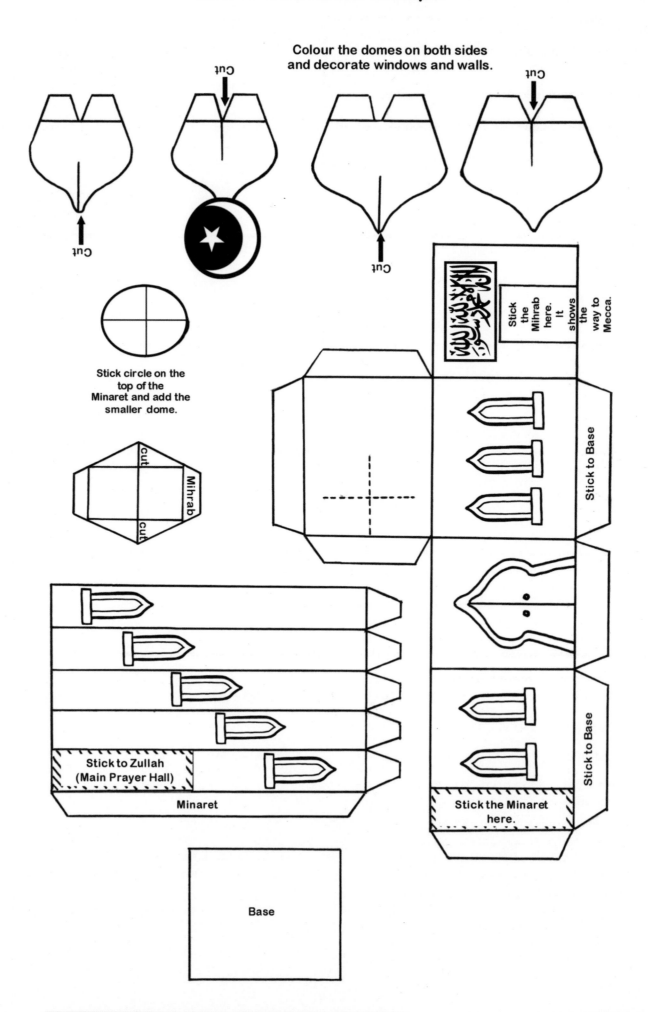

Stick circle on the
top of the
Minaret and add the
smaller dome.

Stick the Mihrab here. It shows the way to Mecca.

Stick to Base

Mihrab

Stick to Base

Stick to Zullah
(Main Prayer Hall)

Minaret

Stick the Minaret
here.

Base

RE Today
Services

REPRESENTING ISLAM: TEN TIPS FOR TEACHERS

Islam

1 Remember that **Islam is a way of life** – not a set of rituals that take place on a special day.

2 Islam is a global religion with a **vast heritage** and has made great contributions in a number of disciplines including art, maths, science, astronomy, literature and medicine. Exploring Muslim artists or scientists is important in representing that history.

Diversity

3 Reflect the **great diversity** of British Islam in teaching – avoid the impression that all Muslims are the same. Muslims in Britain have roots around the world. They do not look the same; they are from many different races, ethnicities and cultures.

4 Not all Muslims practise their faith in identical ways. Different expressions of practice are valid. And remember that **prayer** is more than a set of physical movements and words: just concentrating on the actions can be limiting.

Resources

5 Interactive and engaging resources can and should be used in the teaching of Islam. Use authentic resources from inside the faith community, including artefact, Islamic story, text, websites and books written by Muslims.*

6 Use **resources** which **depict Muslims from all races** and which **challenge negative stereotypes**. Confronting stereotypes with pupils is important. Promoting and managing open discussions can gradually challenge stereotypical notions.

7 Enable children to meet Muslims, but take care with the choices made. If Muslims are not local, then profiling Muslims who are proactive and positive role models (for example Amir Khan, Dr Timothy Winter, Hamza Yusuf, Salma Yaqoob, Yusuf Islam and Nicolas Annelka) is an alternative.

8 Use resources which enable Muslims to speak for themselves. This encourages learning from the experience of the faith community.

9 If you have **Muslim children in your school,** be aware that they may respond in different ways when asked about their faith and culture. Some may be very confident and articulate and welcome the opportunity to share their faith with other pupils. Others may be shy and prefer to keep a low profile when amongst their peers. They should not be used as an authority in the delivery of RE.

In general

10 Make the most of RE's special contribution to whole school issues such as community cohesion. RE should be the lead subject for developing accurate knowledge and understanding of religions and beliefs (Islam in this instance) and for developing positive attitudes of respect and open-mindedness.

Nasima Hassan,
Senior Lecturer,
University of East
London School of
Education

RE and community cohesion

Building community cohesion is about building better relationships between people of different backgrounds. Good RE contributes to building community cohesion by providing opportunities for pupils to:

- **understand and appreciate diversity** by exploring how practices and beliefs vary within traditions, change over time and are influenced by cultures. This could include taking part in visits, speaker events, web-based investigations, dialogues or community projects that involve understanding differences and seeing similarities.

- **evaluate their own and others' beliefs** about why people belong to faith communities, what challenges and tensions might be caused by belonging to a faith, and how religious beliefs relate to a secular worldview.

Source http://www.teachernet.gov.uk/wholeschool/Communitycohesion/communitycohesionresourcepack/tandl/approaches/

See also

* Two examples of the faith community developing high-quality resources to facilitate the teaching of Islam within the primary school are:

- *Books for Schools Project* from the Muslim Council of Britain. http://www.mcb.org.uk/booksforschools.php

- *Citizenship and Muslim Perspectives: Teachers Sharing Ideas* from Islamic Relief in partnership with TIDE (Teachers in Development Education). For more information see: http://www.tidec.org/

ISLAMOPHOBIA - AN ISSUE FOR RE

What is Islamophobia?

Islamophobia is literally translated as the fear of Islam. It is used to refer to prejudice or discrimination against Muslims. The term dates back to the 1980s, but came into common usage after the 11 September attacks in America in 2001.

What causes Islamophobia?

Some of the possible causes are fear, ignorance and the current political climate.

How might it show itself in RE?

- parents not allowing children to go on visits to mosques or take part in activities with Muslim visitors.

- children displaying 'fear' or 'phobia' of Islam for themselves. For some this may develop into hostility or aggression.

- colleagues dismissing Islam as a source for learning from religion.

Issues for teachers

- sensitivity about how Islam is portrayed in school and in wider society

- the intention to give no offence

- pressures on curriculum time in RE.

These and other factors can encourage teachers to 'play safe', and stick to the facts about Islam. This is a shame. Well-planned, imaginative teaching and learning about Islam can lead to:

- ignorance and misinformation being replaced by knowledge and understanding

- children being prepared to think twice about negative media portrayals of Muslims and Islam

- a change of attitude from fear to empathy and respect.

What can I do as the RE subject leader?

- Ask yourself: Would your school deal with Islamophobia more successfully if the advice on page 31 was implemented? Are you already scoring 10 out of 10?

- Challenge media myths about Islam. 'Show Racism the Red Card' have produced an excellent DVD and activity pack which can be used with top primary to adult age groups. For more information go to the Show Racism the Red Card website: http://www.srtrc.org/. The Education Pack of activities to use with the DVD, reproduced with permission of Show Racism the Red Card, is available for download from www.natre.org.uk/cc/#8

- Build teachers' confidence about Islam by providing opportunities for colleagues to meet and get to know local Muslims – ideally those involved in education themselves. Contact your local Standing Advisory Council on RE (SACRE) for contact details.

- For accurate, relevant information about the teachings of Islam on the difficult questions older children and adults may ask, look at the toolkit designed by Monawar Hussain, Imam of Eton College. http://www.teachernet.gov.uk/wholeschool/violentextremism/ompee/

ISLAMOPHOBIA
EDUCATION PACK
To be used in conjunction with the DVD ISLAMOPHOBIA
Show Racism the RED Card